Images of
BATH

The
Bath
Chronicle

Images of
BATH

The Bath Chronicle

Breedon Books
Publishing Company
Derby

First published in Great Britain by
The Breedon Books Publishing Company Limited
44 Friar Gate, Derby, DE1 1DA.
1994

ISBN 1 873626 95 9

Printed and bound by Butler & Tanner, Frome, Somerset.
Covers printed by BDC Printing Services Limited of Derby

Contents

This book is dedicated to the photographers of
The Bath Chronicle who took the great majority of
these pictures over the years.

Foreword

These photographs from *The Bath Chronicle* archives record the changing face of Bath and its people over the years. Some of the changes are so gradual as hardly to be noticed at the time, but photographs taken only a few years apart record them as being substantial. There are also dramatic changes, such as those caused by the ravages of time or the violence and destruction of blitz and flood. A place has been found for all these aspects of the city's life.

Memories fade and vanish as generations pass, but photography has enabled us to preserve some of those memories, the main regret being that photography was invented so late that the city's earlier heyday during its development as a spa and Georgian masterpiece cannot be included although *The Bath Chronicle* has been reporting these events since 1760.

However, photographers, often working with cumbersome and slow plate cameras, have left us a compelling record of our heritage over the past 150 years and it is some of these treasures which we wish to share with our readers now. The photographers remain anonymous because in the main their names are not known, but it is through their initiative and the dangers they sometimes braved that these moments in time have been preserved. As a tribute to them, words have been kept to a minimum so that the images they created may speak for themselves.

David Gledhill
Editor
The Bath Chronicle

The Streets of Bath

Kingston Parade in 1849. In the background, right, are the offices of the *Bath Chronicle* from the 1840s until 1909.

Mineral Water Fountain in Stall Street in 1930. It was here that visitors often had their first taste of Bath spa water.

Motley's Bridge, Twerton, in 1849.

Temperance Hall in Claverton Street. Rudolph Valentino was the heart-throb of the silent movies.

Weigh House in Sawclose.

Market entrance in Market Row, now the Grand Parade.

Twerton in the early 1900s.

The Baroque Rosewell House, Kingsmead Square, in 1910. It was built in 1736.

Royal Avenue in Royal Victoria Park. the park was opened by Princess Victoria 1830 before she became queen.

Laura Fountain, built to mark the centenary of the Bath and West Show in 1877, was replaced by a simpler fountain in 1977 for the bicentenary. On the left is the former Pulteney Hotel, now converted to apartments.

Bridge Street, leading to Pulteney Bridge which was designed by Robert Adam and completed in 1774. It replaced the ferry across the River Avon to Bathwick.

Westgate Street in 1900.

Bush Corner, Kingsmead Square, in 1925. On the left is the entrance to Westgate Buildings.

Walcot Street, Ladymead, with the tramlines leading towards St Michael's Church.

Walcot Street.

Weymouth Street in 1936.
On the right is part of St
James's Church, destroyed
in the blitz of 1942.
Woolworths built a store
on the site of the church
and Weymouth Street. It is
now occupied by
Littlewoods.

Stall Street, leading up to Union Street where the traffic congestion has been solved by making it a
pedestrian precinct.

Arding's
shop in
Union
Street in
1885.

The Terrace Walk area was formerly the centre for city buses.

Terrace Walk and North Parade, leading to York Street. The Royal Literary and Scientific Institution, on the right, was demolished in 1933.

An electric tram in Stall Street. Buses replaced them shortly before World War Two.

Stall Street. The fountain is now in Terrace Walk.

Southgate Street, leading to the Old Bridge. These shop buildings and the bridge have all gone.

Southgate Street, west side from Corn Street to Stall Street in 1931.

Southgate Street, east side, in 1933. The British Home Stores premises now occupy this corner site.

Southgate Street in 1967, before the east side was rebuilt.

Somerset Street in 1933.

Sawclose, at one time known as Timber Green.

Pulteney Street, 1880. Bath chairs wait on the pavement on the left.

Old Bond Street, representing the soot-blackened buildings of Bath before the general clean-up of the stone began in 1953.

North Parade Buildings, formerly Gallaways.

Blacksmith's shop, Newark Street.

Time has not stood still for New Bond Street. The entrance to The Podium now faces the bottom of the street.

Milsom Street looking towards George Street in 1900.

Corner of Milsom Street and Green Street in 1870.

Milsom Street, 1912.

Milsom Street towards George Street in 1914.

Steele and Marsh, chemists, 1920, D.Evans was the proprietor of this Milsom Street business.

Kendall and Sons in Milsom Street.

Milsom Street, 1900.

Lower Borough Walls
looking towards St
James's Church,
destroyed in the 1942
blitz.

High Street showing the Guildhall in 1890, shortly before its extension.

High Street, a view from the Abbey in 1899.

High Street looking towards Cheap Street.

High Street in 1912.

High Street, 25 Bank Chambers and Wilkinson
Engravers in 1868.

High Street, Oliver's boot shop.

Gay Street. The bus is leaving Queen's Parade, formerly the terminus for Bristol.

Hetling Court looking towards Westgate Buildings in 1922.

Green Street in 1933.

Green Street.

George Street.

George Street in 1895.

Dorchester Street. Boots the Chemist and Somerfield are now on the left.

Corn Street in the 1930s.

Corn Street, a large part of which was destined to become a car-park.

Back Street,
north side,
W.J.Holloway.

James' Street West looking towards New Street.

Westgate Place in 1925.

Derrick's Yard between Avon Street and Peter Street.

Archery Ground, Weston Road.

Parked in Park Street.

Pulteney Bridge, part of which had to be rebuilt in 1804 when it began to subside.

King Edward VII memorial in George Street. It now stands in the Parade Gardens.

Grand Parade weirs.

Twerton Weir.

A sluice gate near Pulteney Bridge in 1900.

The Houses of Bath

Old Widcombe Church and Manor, once the home of Horace Vachell, the novelist.

St Catherine Court in 1890.

Widcombe Manor dovecote in 1904.

Widcombe Manor in 1880.

Marshal Wade's house, Abbey Church Yard, in 1904.

Sham Castle in 1870. The folly was built in 1762.

Sham Castle in 1912.

Royal Crescent in 1890. St Andrew's Church in the background was destroyed in the blitz of 1942.

Prior Park College kitchen in the early 1900s.

Prior Park in 1890. The mansion has twice been gutted by fire and twice restored.

Prior Park east wing and terrace in 1870.

Grounds of Prior Park, some of which have been given by the college to the National Trust.

Weir near Prior Park.

Beau Nash house in Sawclose. The home of Bath's most famous master of ceremonies and arbiter of manners later became a restaurant.

Beau Nash house in 1930.

The 16th-century Abbey Church house in 1849.

Abbey Church house in 1885. It was bombed in 1942 and rebuilt.

Abbey Church house in 1910.

Henry Fielding's house, Fielding's Lodge, in 1900. The novelist wrote *The History of Tom Jones, the foundling*.

Rosewell
House.

People & Events

Weston Horticultural show committee, probably taken in the mid 1890s outside the Manor House.

Demolition of the Royal Literary and Scientific Institute in 1932, at the Terrace Walk. It was replaced by underground toilets, the premises being later used as a club.

Demolition of the Royal Literary and Scientific Institute in 1932. It was removed for road improvements.

Demolition of the Royal Literary and Scientific Institute in 1932, seen from the Parade Gardens.

Demolition of the Royal Literary and Scientific Institute in 1932.

Demolition of the Royal Literary and Scientific Institute with Empire Hotel in the background.

Guildhall Market fire in 1972.

Laying of the foundation stone for the Victoria Art Gallery in Bridge Street.

Opening of the Lending Library in 1924 in Bridge Street. Third from the left in the centre row is Mr R.W.M.Wright, the librarian, an authority on Bath's history and also an artist.

Library committee in the 1950s.

Laying the foundation stone for Library and Victoria Art Gallery in 1897, the year of Queen
Victoria's diamond jubilee.

Books being
delivered to
the Municipal
Library.

Reading in the Reference Library in Bridge Street.

Floods in 1894, formerly a familiar feature of city life.

Unveiling of Twerton War Memorial.

Laying the
foundation
stone of the
Church of
Ascension,
South
Twerton, in
1906.

Councillor Major General
Bradshaw's funeral,
leaving St Stephen's
Church.

The John Wood bi-centenary in 1927 at North Parade.

Cleveland Bridge freed of tolls by Lord Bath in 1929.

Lord Bath cuts the tape to free Cleveland Bridge of tolls in 1929.

Lord Bath receives the Freedom of the City in 1930.

Field Marshal Lord Roberts, who saw service in the Indian Mutiny and was Commander-in-Chief of British forces in the Second Boer War, visited the city in 1902.

Mid-Somerset musical competition pictured in the Roman Baths in 1922.

Widcombe Bridge disaster in 1877. Eleven people died when the toll bridge collapsed.

The opening of Laura Fountain.

Winston Churchill arrives in Bath with the then Mayor Kathleen Harper as he receives the Freedom of the City of Bath.

H.T.Warren unveils the tablet to the poet William Wordsworth in North Parade in 1914.

Ladies dressed for the Bath Historical Pageant in 1909. Lady de Blaquière, centre, had the role of Ladye Bath.

Bath Pageant, with Ladye Bath leading her 14 attendants who represented towns in Canada and America named after Bath.

Bath Pageant.

Bath Pageant.

Sir Gilbert Parker unveils the tablet to General Wolfe at 15 Trim Street in 1909. Wolfe was killed when he captured Quebec from the French.

Visit by the Hon W.Reid to unveil a tablet to Edmund Burke at 11 North Parade. The procession is passing down the cobbled Milsom Street.

The visit of Hon W.Reid.

Opening of Dolemeads in 1901.

Lord Rosebery unveiling a tablet to William Pitt at 15 Johnstone Street, which housed the offices of
Bath Conservative Association for many years.

Above: Sir Robert Ball unveils a tablet to the astronomer Sir William Herschel, in New King Street in April 1895.

Left: Lord Rosebery unveils a tablet to the Earl of Chatham at 7 The Circus in 1899.

Mounted section of 212 Wessex RE in 1915.

212 Wessex RE in Victoria Park in 1915.

Officers in the 1st Somerset Rifle Volunteers.

Officers in the 1st Somerset Rifle Volunteers.

Field Marshal Lord French inspects the troops in the High Street in 1915. He was Commander-in-Chief of the British Expeditionary Force to France in 1914.

Lord French and the Mayor outside the Guildhall in 1915. He was in the city to rally support for the war effort and to visit the wounded from the Western Front.

Lord French's visit of 1915, the scene outside the Pump Room.

Lord French on his recruiting drive.

The Baths & Spas

Roman Baths excavations in 1880, after the city's lost past was brought to light in 1878.

Roman Baths excavations.

Roman Baths excavations.

Roman Baths excavation in 1880.

Roman Baths excavations.

Looking at the Roman Baths are George V and Queen Mary and the Mayor of Bath Alderman C.H.Long during the 1917 royal visit.

Roman Baths in 1880.

Circular Baths in 1890.

Roman Baths with now demolished buildings behind it south of the Abbey.

Roman Baths in 1900 as it began to take its present appearance.

King's Bath in 1890.

King's Bath in 1900.

The Old Royal Bath, or Hot Bath, on the right leading to the Cross Bath.

King's and Queen's Baths, Stall Street entrance in 1890 with a Bath chair in a doorway.

Cold Bath House at Widcombe.

The Pump Room

Pump Room orchestra, Frank Comez and his octet in 1939.

The Pump Room Terrace in 1900.

Taking tea on the Pump Room terrace in 1925.

The Pump Room Terrace in 1914.

The Drawing room at the Pump Room in 1900.

The Pump Room spa water fountain in 1920.

The Pump Room, social centre for tea, dances and other entertainments, especially musical.

The Pump Room, elegantly furnished.

The Pump Room, still splendid in proportions and decoration but rather less elegantly furnished.

The Pump Room fountain showing the area reserved for subscribers.

The Pump Room Colonnade and façade in 1925, seen from the Grand Pump Room Hotel.

The Pump Room showing Bath chairs in 1900. They continued in use until the 1930s.

The Pump Room showing Bath chairs in 1900.

View of the Pump Room before the Concert Hall extension was built, taken in 1896.

Churches & Chapels

A rather self-conscious group pose for the camera outside Portland Chapel.

Ebenezor Chapel and Waterloo Buildings.

Bathwick Chapel.

Widcombe Cemetery in 1890.

All Saints' Chapel, Lansdown, in 1890. It opened in 1794 and was burnt out in the blitz of 1942.

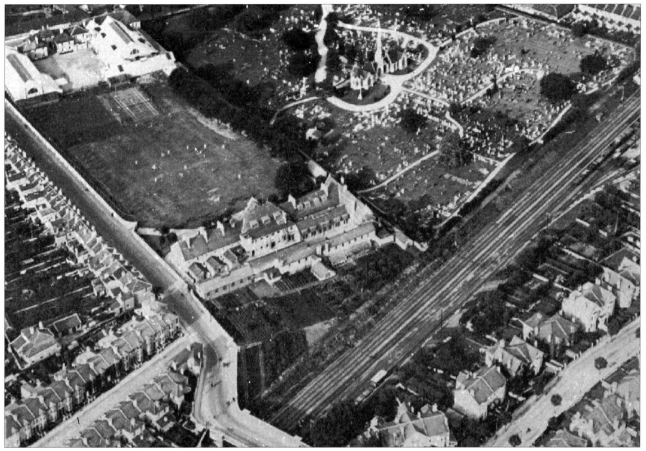

St James's Cemetery on the Lower Bristol Road.

Batheaston Church in 1860.

St Mary's Chapel,
Queen Square,
which was
demolished in the
1870s to make way
for road
improvements.

Argyle Chapel in 1910.

Judas tree at St Mary Magdalene, Holloway.

St Stephen's Church, Lansdown.

St John's Church at South Parade. The orchard in the foreground is now the site of the police station and a car-park.

St James's Church at the junction of Stall Street and Southgate.

St James's Church in 1849.

The Rev Mr Heard with scenes showing the inside and outside of St Michael's Church.

Trinity Church, James Street West, was consecrated in 1822 but did not survive the blitz of 1942.

St Michael's Church.

St Michael's Church in 1880. The Post Office now stands on the site at the left of the picture.

St Michael's Church, with cables for the electric trams showing clearly.

St Mary's Church, Bathwick, taken in 1900.

St John the Baptist Church, Bathwick.

St John's, Bathwick, in 1890.

St Andrew's Church in Julian Road. Its blitzed site is now just an open triangular green.

St Andrew's Church, with cars parked at the rear of the Royal Crescent.

Bath Abbey, view from the river in 1890.

Bath Abbey looking from the river over Parade Gardens.

Bath Abbey, the view from the south-east in 1890.

Bath Abbey, the view from the Parade Gardens in 1932.

Bath Abbey and the Empire Hotel.

Bath Abbey looking over Orange Grove in 1890.

Bath Abbey from the Grand Parade.

Bath Abbey from Orange Grove in 1880.

Bath Abbey from Orange Grove in 1890.

Interior of Prior Park Chapel, some years after building work was abandoned during a temporary closure of the school. It was later completed, apart from the fluting of some columns and is one of the little-known glories of Bath.

Royal Occasions & Celebrations

Bath Abbey floodlit during the Coronation celebrations in 1937.

Milsom Street decorated for the diamond jubilee of Queen Victoria in 1897.

HRH the Prince of Wales visits the Roman Baths in 1923.

Princess Marina, Duchess of Kent, visits the city in 1938 for the reopening of the Assembly Rooms.

Crowds gather outside the Royal Baths during the visit of the Duchess of Kent in 1938.

Milsom Street decorated for the Coronation of Edward VII in 1902.

The Guildhall at the time of the Coronation of Edward VII.

The 1887 golden jubilee of Queen Victoria celebrations outside Bath Church Institute.

Crowds turned out to cheer when King George V visited the city on 17 November 1917, as World War One approached its climax.

King George V inspects a guard of honour during his visit.

George V in Stall Street during his 1917 visit.

Glistening boots
on a muddy
November day as
King George V
inspects a
detachment of his
troops.

Proclamation of King George V at the Guildhall in 1910.

King George V Coronation celebrations.

Three cheers for King George V at his Coronation celebrations.

Proclamation of King George V in May of 1910.

King George V Coronation decorations in Bridge Street.

King George V Coronation arches in Milsom Street.

The Pump Room was festooned with flags and flowers for the Coronation of King George V.

Queen Victoria's diamond jubilee celebrations, 1897.

Men about town in Milsom Street at the time of the 1897 diamond jubilee celebrations.

Fashion and bunting during the 1897 diamond jubilee celebrations.

Pedestrians could walk the streets in safety in 1897.

Diamond jubilee bunting in Southgate Street, the building all now swept away.

Flags came out for the jubilee celebrations in High Street.

Roasting an ox for the jubilee celebrations in Victoria Park.

Crowds thronged Victoria Park for the jubilee festivities.

Shops bid to out-do each other during the jubilee celebrations.

Civic Splendour

The Banqueting Room at the Guildhall pictured *c.*1900.

Bath City Council in 1911, when Mr J.Plowman was Mayor.

Bath Guildhall in
stereoscope in 1870.

Bath Guildhall in 1892.

Bath Guildhall in 1895.

The Bath Blitz

Children suddenly found water was a precious commodity when the city was blitzed for two nights in April 1942.

Smouldering ruins after two nights of destruction in which more than 400 people were killed.

The homeless were given tea from mobile canteens. More than 19,000 properties were destroyed or damaged.

The slogan said Dig for Victory Now, but the priority that day was to dig for casualties.

Julian Road, ravaged by explosives and fire.

Battered Lansdown Place East.

Shattered houses stretched into Lansdown Crescent from Lansdown Place East.

Life, for most, went on with newspapers in high demand.

Canteens were set up to feed the homeless and emergency services.

Washing at the Roman Baths.

After the rubble was cleared this derelict site blossomed into the city's new bus station at Manvers Street.

The Bear Flat was almost totally destroyed.

Bear Flat shops with their fronts blown in.

Searching in the rubble for survivors.

Troops guarded the remains of the Bank of England at the Bear Flat.

Rescuers risked their lives from collapsing buildings as they dug for survivors.

More than 30 guests and staff died when a bomb hit the Regina Hotel opposite the Assembly Rooms.

An air-raid shelter still stands at the end of the table in this Dartmouth Avenue celebration.

The Bath Floods

The Bath Floods of 1882. A raft came in useful for crossing James Street West.

The River Avon in full flood in 1960. The piers of the Old Bridge were partly blamed for holding back the water and shortly afterwards the bridge was demolished and the Churchill Bridge built further downstream.

Clearing up the damage caused by the 1960 flooding.

Police and firemen help rescue people during the 1960 flooding.

One way for one person at least to
keep his feet dry.

Looking up Southgate Street during the 1960 floods.

Helping hands for stranded drivers as the Avon swept into Bath in 1960.

Sandbags were
used in a mostly
vain attempt to
keep the river
water at bay.

'Hang on a minute, we're coming'.

Trams & Transport

Bathampton ferry with ferryman in foreground in 1870.

Electric trams in Southgate in 1925 with their uncovered upper decks.

An electric tram in
Kingsmead Square.

A tram near the tram depot in Walcot Street.

Trams in Kingsmead Square in 1925.

Healing the Sick

St Catherine's Hospital where the 14 women inmates had to be over 55.

Southern Dispensary, Claverton Street.

The then soot-stained St John's Hospital, West Side, in 1941.

The United Hospital in Beau Street in 1849, 23 years after it opened. The building budget was £5,000 for this union of the City Infirmary and the Casualty Hospital.

The United Hospital, also in 1849. When the Royal United Hospital was built at Combe Park the hospital building became Bath Technical College.

Lessons Learnt

The new South Twerton School which was opened in 1893.

Twerton Parochial School at the turn of the century.

Pupils from Twerton Parochial School grouped on the pavement.

Boys in school uniform.

Old Blue Coat School in Sawclose.

Blue Coat schoolboys in 1896.

Waiting for children outside Twerton Parochial School.

St James's School South.

It all seems innocent enough, but the police were there just in case.

Children at fair ground.

Hotels & Pubs

Hotels come and go. This one went.

Crown and Anchor in Weston.

The Royal Sailor at the foot of Holloway and Wells Road was pulled down for road improvements.

The High Street once had six inns. This one went from the Guildhall extension into Bridge Street.

White Hart in Stall Street. It was demolished to make room for the Grand Pump Room Hotel which opened in 1869.

The George Inn at Bathampton.

Pulteney Hotel and Laura Fountain in 1910 when the heyday of the horse-drawn cabs was drawing to a close.

Pulteney Hotel and Laura Fountain in 1912.

Pulteney Street, Bath, looking back with Laura Fountain in the foreground.

Royal York Hotel in 1849. Princess Victoria stayed there.

Westgate Street in 1900.

Seven Dials Inn in 1936.

Saracen's Head
in Broad Street,
1912.

Three Cups in
Walcot Street.

Beehive pub in
Walcot Street in
1936.

Grand Pump Room Hotel in 1897. It was demolished in 1958 to make way for the Arlington House
shops and apartments.

Grand Pump
Room Hotel in
1910. It was
ideally sited for
guests having
spa treatment.

Grand Pump Room Hotel in 1912.

Grand Pump Room Hotel in 1930 within nine years it was to be requisitioned by the Admiralty for the duration of World War Two.

Full Moon Hotel at Old Bridge. It was replaced by the offices of the electricity company in the early 1930s.

Empire Hotel with Bath's former police station on the left.

Bridge Street when horses were still in competition with cars.

Subscribers

Mr W Aldred
Pamela Allen
Mr & Mrs V L Andrew
William James Baker
Mr Joe Barr
Stephen Bletso
Vera Bolland
M C & H J Bond
Miss Jill Bowen
Dr & Mrs C E Boyd
Beryl Brooks
Stanley A Brown
Mark Bryant
Mr Roger K Bryant
Mr W L Burt
R Butcher
Barry Carter
Dr E Cheah
E Chesterman
Trevor Chirgwin
Alan Cobb
Miss Cynthia Cook
Mrs Rosalie Critchley
Bruce D Crofts
B Croker
Mrs Audrey Dawson
Linda & Jim Dennis
Jennifer Dixon
Mr R H Dodd
Mr R Dolman
Mrs M A Doman
Vera Dyer
Mr L L Edwards
Paul Elliott
Mrs M Ennor
Mr Euellane
Mr & Mrs A E Evans
Jill Fenwick
Mrs Betty Fews
Dr & Mrs R J K Fleming
Mrs Jean Freeman
Wanda & Peter French
Margaret Gardner
John H Goulding
Gillian Green
Mike Gutteridge
Elizabeth Haddock
Michael J Hall
Mrs E A Hancock
Mr S Hardy
Mr Guy Harper
Mr & Mrs H A Harrell
Davis Hawkins
Mrs K G Heavens
Mr Patrick Henderson
S M Hodges
John Holness
Jon Hursey
G M Iles/Lloyds Bank
Derek Jerome
June M Johns
Mrs Kirkup

Mr D R Kite
Mrs G Letts
Marek Lewcun & Anita Butera
Mr M F Lewis
Derek G Lovell
Frank McAteer
Rodger R McSorley
Molly Magner
Mrs Ann V Marchant
Anne Marks
John Edward Marks
Wendy Marriott
Lynn May
Mrs S Miller
Iris Moger
Captain & Mrs D Mordaunt
John A Mudford
J & B Niblett
Rachel Novak
Mr R Odey
Harvey & Patsy
Raymond Pattemore
Mr V M Peplow
Colin Peters
Gwenda Peters
Leslie J Pink
Barbara M Piper
Mrs R Plumley
Mr D E Pow
A Powlesland
Robert & Gillian Rawlings
Mr & Mrs F D Rich
Kenneth C Richmond
Mrs J Ridley
Mr & Mrs Rugg
Joanna M Ryan
Mr R Salisbury
Martin & Maureen Schueler
Mrs M J Seviour
Charles Sheppard
Mrs J Sims
Brian & Rosemary Smith
C G Sperring
D H Stennard
Chris & Graham Targett
E M Taylor
Mr K F Taylor
Mr Peter Taylor
Jonathan Tettel
K P I Timmis
Mrs P Thomas
Mr R Thomas
Mr Jack Tooze
Mr Roger M Walter
G F K Ward
Mr D Weston
Mr & Mrs R J Whatley
F Wiles
Mrs Shirley Williams
Mr I Willshire
R Woolford
Mrs K Yeomans